The Life Cycle of a
Kangaroo
by Lisa Trumbauer

Consulting Editor: Gail Saunders-Smith, Ph.D.

Consultant: Daniel T. Blumstein, Ph.D., Assistant Professor
Department of Organismic Biology, Ecology, and Evolution
University of California, Los Angeles

Pebble Books

an imprint of Capstone Press
Mankato, Minnesota

Pebble Books are published by Capstone Press
151 Good Counsel Drive, P.O. Box 669, Mankato, Minnesota 56002
www.capstonepress.com

1 2 3 4 5 6 07 06 05 04 03 02

Library of Congress Cataloging-in-Publication Data
Trumbauer, Lisa, 1963–
    The life cycle of a kangaroo / by Lisa Trumbauer.
    p. cm.—(Life cycles)
    Summary: Simple text and photographs present the life cycle of the kangaroo.
    Includes bibliographical references (p. 23) and index.
    ISBN-13: 978-0-7368-1452-2 (hardcover)
    ISBN-10: 0-7368-1452-3 (hardcover)
    ISBN-13: 978-0-7368-3396-7 (softcover pbk.)
    ISBN-10: 0-7368-3396-X (softcover pbk.)
    1. Kangaroos—Life cycles—Juvenile literature. [1. Kangaroos.] I. Title. II. Life
cycles (Mankato, Minn.)
QL737.M35 T78 2003
599.2′22—dc21   2002001223

Note to Parents and Teachers

The Life Cycles series supports national science standards related to
life science. This book describes and illustrates the life cycle of a red
kangaroo. The photographs support early readers in understanding
the text. The repetition of words and phrases helps early readers learn
new words. This book also introduces early readers to subject-specific
vocabulary words, which are defined in the Words to Know section.
Early readers may need assistance to read some words and to use the
Table of Contents, Words to Know, Read More, Internet Sites, and
Index/Word List sections of the book.

(Table of Contents

Photographs in this book show the life cycle of a red kangaroo.

7 days

A kangaroo begins life as a pouch young. A pouch young looks like a tiny worm.

1 month

The pouch young lives
inside its mother's pouch.
It drinks milk from
her body.

5 months

8

The pouch young grows and changes. Fur grows on its body.

The young kangaroo
is now called a joey.
The joey can poke its
head out of the pouch.

6 months

The joey can first leave the pouch after about six months. The mother and joey live with a group called a mob.

1 year

The joey grows too big for the pouch. It stays with its mother for about one year. The young kangaroo is now called a young-at-foot.

A young-at-foot becomes an adult when it is about two years old. Kangaroos can live up to 20 years.

A female kangaroo mates with a male kangaroo. She gives birth to a pouch young after about one month.

joey

young-at-foot

pouch young

adult

The pouch young is the start of a new life cycle.

Words to Know

joey—a young kangaroo that lives in its mother's pouch

life cycle—the stages of life of an animal; the life cycle includes being born, growing up, having young, and dying.

mate—to join together to produce young

mob—a group of kangaroos that lives together; from two to 20 kangaroos live in a mob.

pouch—a part of a female kangaroo's body in which a young kangaroo lives and grows

pouch young—a young kangaroo that has just been born; a pouch young is about the size of a jellybean.

young-at-foot—a young kangaroo that has outgrown its mother's pouch but still lives with her

Read More

Burt, Denise. *Kangaroos.* Minneapolis: Carolrhoda Books, 2000.

Lever, E. Melanie. *Kangaroos.* Animals Are Fun! Milwaukee: Gareth Stevens, 2000.

Whitehouse, Patricia. *Kangaroo.* Zoo Animals. Chicago: Heinemann Library, 2002.

Internet Sites

FactHound offers a safe, fun way to find Internet sites related to this book.

Go to *www.facthound.com*

He'll fetch the best sites for you!

FactHound will fetch the best sites for you!

Index/Word List

Word Count: 155
Early-Intervention Level: 15

Editorial Credits

Martha E. H. Rustad, editor; Kia Adams, cover designer; Jennifer Schonborn, interior designer; Wanda Winch, photo researcher; Karen Risch, product planning editor

Photo Credits

Bruce Coleman Inc./Norman Owen Tomalin, 12
Minden Pictures/Frans Lanting, cover (left), 1; Mitsuaki Iwago, 4, 6, 8, 10, 14, 16, 18, 20 (all)
Photo Network/Chad Ehlers, cover (right)